Gerhard Domagk and the Discovery of Sulfa

John Bankston

Mitchell Lane
PUBLISHERS

PO Box 619
Bear, Delaware 19701

Unlocking the Secrets of Science

Profiling 20th Century Achievers in Science, Medicine, and Technology

Gerhard Domagk and the Discovery of Sulfa

Copyright © 2003 by Mitchell Lane Publishers, Inc. All rights reserved. No part of this book may be reproduced without written permission from the publisher. Printed and bound in the United States of America.

Printing   1   2   3   4   5   6   7   8   9

Library of Congress Cataloging-in-Publication Data

Bankston, John, 1974-
    Gerhard Domagk and the discovery of sulfa/John Bankston.
       p. cm. — (Unlocking the secrets of science)
    Summary: A biography of the German scientist responsible for developing the use of sulfa as an antibiotic in the early twentieth century.
    Includes bibliographical references and index.
    ISBN 1-58415-115-3 (library)
    1. Domagk, Gerhard, 1895-1964—Juvenile literature. 2. Sulphur drugs—History—Juvenile literature. 3. Antibacterial agents—History—Juvenile literature. 4. Medical scientists—Germany—Biography—Juvenile literature. [1. Domagk, Gerhard, 1895-1964. 2. Scientists. 3. Sulphur drugs—History.] I. Series.
RM666.S9 D653 2003
615'.2723—dc21
[B]   2002019056

ABOUT THE AUTHOR: Born in Boston, Massachusetts, John Bankston began publishing articles in newspapers and magazines while still a teenager. Since then, he has written over two hundred articles, and contributed chapters to books such as *Crimes of Passion* and *Death Row 2000*, which have been sold in bookstores around the world. He has recently written a number of biographies for Mitchell Lane including books on Mandy Moore, Jessica Simpson and Jonas Salk. He has worked as a writer for the movies Dot-Com and the upcoming *Planetary Suicide*, which begins filming in 2002. As an actor John has appeared in episodes of *Sabrina the Teenage Witch*, *Charmed* and *Get Real* along with appearances in the films *Boys and Girls*, and *America So Beautiful*. He has a supporting part in *Planetary Suicide* and has recently completed his first young adult novel, *18 To Look Younger*.

CHILDREN'S SCIENCE REVIEWER: Stephanie Kondrchek, B.S. Microbiology, University of Maryland

PHOTO CREDITS: cover: Corbis; p. 6 Corbis; pp. 10, 14, 18, 19, 20, 24, 33, 36, 37, 41, 42 Corbis; p. 30 Science Photo Library; p. 38 Hulton Archive; p. 43 AP Photo.

PUBLISHER'S NOTE: In selecting those persons to be profiled in this series, we first attempted to identify the most notable accomplishments of the 20th century in science, medicine, and technology. When we were done, we noted a serious deficiency in the inclusion of women. For the greater part of the 20th century science, medicine, and technology were male-dominated fields. In many cases, the contributions of women went unrecognized. Women have tried for years to be included in these areas, and in many cases, women worked side by side with men who took credit for their ideas and discoveries. Even as we move forward into the 21st century, we find women still sadly underrepresented. It is not an oversight, therefore, that we profiled mostly male achievers. Information simply does not exist to include a fair selection of women.

Contents

Gerhard Domagk, the German scientist who discovered the antibiotic properties of sulfa is shown in this 1930s photo.

Chapter 1
Almost Forgotten

●●●

T he stories of their lives fill bookshelves. When they were alive, they were as celebrated as movie stars, as recognized as the president. They were the doctors who produced treatments for some of the deadliest diseases, the scientists whose innovations ushered in the space age. Even today, many of them are still world famous.

Medical miracles from the 20th century, such as Jonas Salk's polio vaccine and Alexander Fleming's discovery of penicillin, are still being used in the 21st century. In his last years of life, Fleming was widely recognized for his work with penicillin. Meanwhile, Salk lived for several decades after his discovery and gained enormous publicity from his triumphs.

However, the work of some scientific and medical pioneers offered only brief benefits before later, more long-lasting discoveries overshadowed them. The ideas of these lesser-known pioneers bridged gaps in history, providing life-saving treatments when none were available. Their cures were like bottle rockets, exploding into use before quickly fading away.

Despite their lack of fame, these men and women made vital contributions to the 20th century. Their discoveries paved the way for later innovations while saving thousands of lives in the process. This is the story of one of these early 20th-century pioneers. He discovered a drug that preceded penicillin for fighting deadly bacteria.

Currently, modern medicine relies on antibiotics to destroy agents of infection while saving the patient. Bacteria causes many infections and diseases. Preventing the growth of these organisms can be traced back to the work of 19th century scientists, such as Louis Pasteur and Paul Ehrlich. Fleming discovered the miracle of penicillin when he noticed a strain of it growing in an unwashed petri dish.

Penicilliums are part of the fungi family that includes mushrooms and mold. John Tyndall first noted their bacteria fighting ability in the 1870s. D.A. Gratia in 1925 noticed this as well. Fleming's experiments paved the way for modern penicillin three years later. Still, the penicillium Fleming experimented with wasn't widely used as a medical treatment for nearly two decades after its discovery. Before then, soldiers and surgeons used another drug, later known as sulfa.

Sulfa and penicillin can fight organisms so small over a billion of them could fit in a teaspoon of dirt. French scientist Pasteur first theorized in 1865 that specific germs caused specific diseases. These germs were microscopic single-celled organisms called bacteria. A few years later, German scientist Robert Koch developed bacteriology, a new branch of medicine devoted to studying more than 2500 different types of these tiny organisms.

Most bacteria are harmless, even helpful. Unfortunately, a few can be deadly. One of the most-infamous harmful ones is the *Streptococcus pyogenes* bacteria. This organism grows in long chains and, as does all bacteria, reproduces by cell division. This means it splits in half, then one cell becomes two, two become four, and so on. Since bacterial cell division can occur every 20 minutes, streptococcus spreads quickly.

Today, the bacteria is best known as the cause of strep throat, an infection quite common in children. Strep throat is highly contagious and often spreads when an infected person sneezes or coughs. Fortunately, this illness is very treatable today. Before the 1900s, infection by the streptococcus often was deadly.

Besides the dangers of strep throat, even minor injuries were susceptible to this bacteria. A century ago, the tiniest infected cut could become fatal. In wartime, another bacteria called the *Clostridium welchii* could be as deadly for soldiers as the *Streptococcus pyogenes* was for civilians. The clostridium produces seed-like spores that can survive for years and are responsible for a grave condition known as gas gangrene.

During combat, shrapnel, or pieces of an exploding bomb or other artillery, can injure soldiers. Sometimes bits of dirty clothing, ground debris and even vegetation carrying the *Clostridium welchii* bacteria also enter the wound. The bacteria creates a gas gangrene infection that spreads along the muscle, if left untreated, turning the affected area black and expanding it with gas. Before the 1920s, the only way to save a soldier's life from this type of infection was through amputation, or cutting off the infected arm or leg. Even then, the wounded soldier often died.

Finding a solution to the bacteria riddle was a difficult task for early 20th century scientists. How do you eliminate bad bacteria without also harming the patient? While dozens tried to find the answer, the work of one man provided the clearest solution for the times. Surprisingly, the answer didn't come from the world of medicine; it came from industry. A red dye called Prontosil used to stain leather became a primary ingredient for sulfa.

The man who discovered Prontosil's anti-bacterial properties used sulfa to save the lives of England's Prime Minister and the son of a U.S. president. He even used the drug to save the life of his own daughter. During the peak use of sulfa, the drug saved the lives of both soldiers and civilians. Despite his accomplishments, the man's contribution to modern medicine has been largely forgotten. The man's name was Gerhard Domagk, and this is his story.

Louis Pasteur, shown here, said, "Chance favors only the prepared mind." Gerhard Domagk strongly believed this statement. Domagk wanted to pursue medical research, joining a new generation of doctors working to cure illnesses, rather than just treat them.

Chapter 2

The Changing World

• •

L ying beneath the shadows of an ancient castle, across the water from a rustic lake, the Domagk family home was more than a place to live. It also served as a schoolhouse to neighborhood students in the rural town of Lagow. The town was set in the scenic Brandenburg Marches, a region now part of Poland, in Eastern Europe. When Gerhard Johannes Paul Domagk was born on October 30, 1895, the region was still part of Germany.

While Gerhard was a toddler, the blue-eyed tow-head often watched mesmerized as his father Paul taught in their home. Although the short trip from his bedroom to his father's classroom probably appealed to the young Gerhard, by the time he was old enough to attend school, his father already had taken another job.

Paul became a teacher and assistant headmaster, similar to a vice principal, at a grammar school in nearby Sommerfield. Although many of the businesses in Sommerfield were clothing factories, the region surrounding the town's center was dominated by family farms that were centuries old. In fact, Gerhard's mother, Martha Reimer, was the daughter of one of Sommerfield's more prominent farming families.

Despite his family roots, no one ever truly thought that the quietly curious Gerhard would grow up to be a farmer. Like many European schools, the ones near the Domagk home tested students when they were very young. Elementary school children were placed in schools designed to maximize their talents. Gerhard's test scores in math and science were very high. They enabled him to attend the school where his father taught. It specialized in science and offered students the best possible learning environment to prepare them for careers as future doctors and scientists.

Gerhard took a path similar to many young people in the early 20th century. The world he grew up in was changing more rapidly than ever before. Although many innovations—from electricity to motor cars—were slow to reach rural areas like Gerhard's birthplace, other developments had a great deal of impact on families like the Domagks. The rise of factories during the Industrial Revolution caused many countries, such as Germany and the United States, to move from rural, farm-based economies to urban, manufacturing ones. Improvements in farming techniques also decreased the need for young men to become farmers. These young people often moved away from home, pursuing careers and lifestyles their parents couldn't even imagine.

Even as a young teen, Gerhard dreamed of the world beyond the Marches. He longed for a place where scientific discoveries changed the world of medicine as quickly as innovations, such as the assembly line, transformed the world of manufacturing.

Already, sophisticated microscopes had altered how scientists studied cells. In the 19th century, Pasteur's germ theory of disease explained how germs cause most infectious diseases. This discovery led to the science of microbiology, the branch of biology dealing with microscopic forms of life.

"Chance favors only the prepared mind," Pasteur once said. Gerhard strongly believed this statement. He wanted to pursue medical research, joining a new generation of scientists and doctors working to cure illnesses rather than just treat them.

Although he wanted to be a doctor, Gerhard did not want to make house calls. He saw little value in offering ineffective medicines and kind words to dying patients.

Instead, Gerhard saw himself among researchers who changed medicine forever in the 20th century.

In 1909, Gerhard began attending secondary school at Leignitz in the town of Silesia. After graduation, he was accepted to the medical program at the University of Kiel. This school, established by the Duke Christian Albrecht of Schleswig-Holstein Gottorf in 1665, had expanded considerably in the late 1800s. By the time Gerhard arrived, the university's medical program was recognized as one of the best in Germany.

Unfortunately, 1914 wasn't the best year to begin attending college in Europe. Another development from the modern age, advanced warfare, quickly interrupted Gerhard's studies. While wars have existed as long as people have formed societies, the dawn of the 20th century brought the widespread use of chemical weapons, machine guns, tanks, and airplanes. The devastation wrought by this new technology would be unlike any seen before.

And Gerhard Domagk was about to witness it firsthand.

During World War I, thousands of wounded soldiers died from infections. There were no antibiotics available at that time.

Chapter 3

The Great War

• •

Gerhard had barely graduated from high school when the Great War tore apart the world he knew. World War I began when an assassin killed the heir to the throne of Austria-Hungry, the Archduke Franz Ferdinand, in the summer of 1914. While the event was scarcely noticed in many parts of the world, it set in motion a series of events that would cost millions of lives.

Austria suspected that Serbia supported the assassin, so Austria responded by making demands on Serbia. When Serbia's response was hostile, Austria declared war. The move cut short Gerhard's enrollment in the medical program at the University of Kiel. Because Germany was an ally of Austria, when Austria declared war, Germany pledged its support. Since Russia was allied with Serbia, it quickly sent troops to the Russian-Austrian border. Before the conflict ended on Nov. 11, 1918, most of Europe, along with Canada and the United States became involved.

For Gerhard, the war had immediate consequences. Soldiers were fighting and dying not far from Lagow. By the fall of 1914, many regions of Europe had become battlefields. Gerhard didn't believe he had a choice about getting involved in the war. He had to fight.

He wasn't alone. In the early months of the war, many of Gerhard's classmates joined him in volunteering for duty. Even before the 20th century, college men have managed to avoid active service. However, for German students this wasn't an option. The Great War was different. For many of them, the soldiers were fighting in the fields of their hometowns. They couldn't just go to class and ignore it. Educated men, such as Gerhard, had less dangerous options, such as enrolling in officer training programs. Gerhard refused to take the safest path. He was healthy and active, a lean man, six-feet-tall, who believed his duty was clear. He would serve in combat.

Gerhard dropped out of college and joined a student army where he trained with many of his peers. He became part of the Leibgrenadier Regiment of Frankfort on the Oder. This was an elite unit of specially selected foot soldiers trained in launching grenades.

The battles required to win a war are always horrible, but the ones Gerhard witnessed were especially tragic. Many were fought from giant, lengthy holes dug into the ground called trenches. Large waves of men would climb out of the trenches and attack the enemy, only to have machine gun fire mow them down. Chemical weapons, such as mustard gas that slowly destroys the lungs and takes weeks to kill its victims, were also used, mainly by the Germans. Gerhard witnessed many of these tragedies, first in the battle of Langemarck and then in late 1914 when he was transferred to the eastern front of Europe.

There, Gerhard fought on one of World War I's most famous battlefields; the Flanders section of what later became Belgium. John McCrae immortalized the thousands of men who died in this tragic location in the poem "In Flanders Fields."

"In Flanders fields the poppies blow
Between the crosses, row on row,
That mark our place; and in the sky
The larks, still bravely singing, fly
Scarce heard amid the guns below."

Gerhard's time as a soldier at Flanders came to an abrupt conclusion when he was wounded in December of

1914, and sent to a hospital to recover. He was one of the lucky ones. Gerhard survived his injuries. But all around him, men were dying from a particularly vicious bacterial infection known as gas gangrene.

Most of Gerhard's fellow soldiers were like him, still teenagers. They arrived at the hospital in dirty uniforms, their wounds barely treated. What others would later realize is that the clothing these soldiers wore was responsible for the infections that often led to amputations and even death. Their tattered uniforms were breeding grounds for the *Clostridium welchii* bacteria that causes deadly gas gangrene, and the *Clostridium tetani* bacteria that causes lock jaw and other dangerous muscle spasms. Both bacteria live in horses' intestines and survive in the manure that littered the fields where the soldiers fought.

Gerhard's familiarity with the diseases caused by bacteria only grew after his recovery. Instead of returning to his unit, he volunteered with the Army Medical Group, joining a division called the Sanitary Service. As part of this group, his primary job was preventing infections he encountered while in an army hospital.

Unfortunately, the techniques for killing the bacteria often did as much damage as the disease. In the early 1900s, the primary method was using antiseptics. Septic comes from the Greek word for rotten and was first used in a medical sense by Sir John Pringle in 1750. Pringle was a wartime physician who noted how wounds became rotted and suggested antiseptics to fight the rot. Nearly 50 years before World War I, Joseph Lister among others realized microorganisms, such as bacteria, caused this rot. This discovery prompted surgeons to become far more careful about germs. They began wearing sterile operating gowns, masks and eventually gloves.

Joseph Lister recognized that microorganisms, such as bacteria, caused infection. This discovery prompted surgeons to be far more careful about germs.

It was Lister who recommended the use of antiseptics that could kill germs but not living tissues. Unfortunately, Lister's antiseptic was a highly diluted carbolic acid that was ineffective in treating those injured in combat. Infectious bacteria was driven too deeply into a wound to be affected.

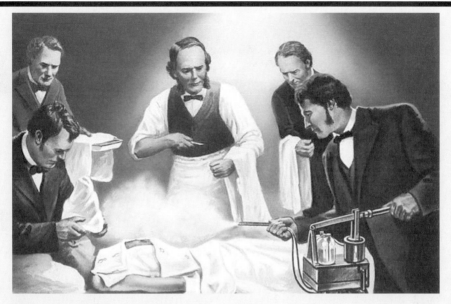

This painting shows Lister spraying an antiseptic over a patient to help disinfect the area that was to be operated on.

Gerhard was one of a number of men struggling to save soldiers' lives during World War I who realized how ineffective the technique was. Unfortunately, it was the best treatment available to the medical men of the German Army. As the German forces moved into Russia, giant mobile hospitals were set up to receive the wounded. Gerhard was assigned to one of these, where he dealt with another infectious epidemic called cholera. This acute intestinal infection caused by the bacterium *Vibrio cholerae* swept through large portions of war-ravaged Russia with devastating results. In some areas, more soldiers died from this disease than from battle.

The suffering Gerhard witnessed moved him tremendously. After watching powerlessly as hundreds of men died from an enemy both invisible and deadly, he knew what he would do when the war ended. He would save lives by developing solutions to the deadly bacteria riddle.

Paul Ehrlich was a German doctor who was awarded the Nobel Prize for Physiology or Medicine in 1908 for his work in immunology. Ehrlich crafted a vaccine that kills syphilis microbes without harming the patient.

Chapter 4

The Road Back

• •

World War I was called the war to end all wars. Those who experienced the conflict prayed the same atrocities never would be repeated. When Germany signed the Armistice peace treaty on November 11, 1918, Europe was a vastly different continent.

The war had devastated Germany. Nearly two million of its young men died in the conflict. By contrast, the United States, who became involved near the end of the war, lost less than 100,000 soldiers. All told, nearly 10 million people died during World War I.

Despite the losses, Germany only surrendered from fear of revolution. The year before, Russia fell to the communists, and as the conflict dragged on, the citizens of Germany seemed equally hungry for change. By agreeing to end the war, Germany also consented to a number of conditions, including payments to countries they had bombed. The payments crippled the country financially. In addition, the 1919 Treaty of Versailles altered borders, cementing the existence of Poland. Over the following several years, Poland came to include many areas where Gerhard grew up.

Despite the changes, politics concerned Gerhard less than education. He reenrolled in 1918 at the University of Kiel and resumed his medical school studies. Although he'd returned to a region devastated by war, and a country suffering greatly under the terms of its surrender, Gerhard was not daunted. He didn't let his homeland's problems overshadow important new opportunities for him.

The class Gerhard joined was ready for post-war life. Many of his classmates shared Gerhard's background, fighting as soldiers or serving in the medical corp. They were older than most students, and a little bit wiser.

This time Gerhard's education was uninterrupted. He devoted himself to both basic medical subjects and research. He particularly was interested in creatine. For his thesis, he wrote a paper on how people lose creatine when they sweat following vigorous physical activity. This nutrient, first discovered in 1832, accumulates in the muscles as a result of exercise. (Recently, it has become a very popular diet supplement for bodybuilders and other active people.)

After taking his state examinations in medicine, Gerhard received his M.D. degree in 1921. Most of his graduating class went on to practice medicine or become surgeons, but Gerhard was interested far more in discovery. He took a position as an assistant to chemist Ernst Felix Hoppe-Seyler, the namesake of a famous scientist at the University of Greifswald who, during the 1800s, had done ground-breaking research into the chemical properties of hemoglobin (part of red blood cells).

In 1923, Gerhard moved to Greifswald where he worked at the Pathological Institute under the supervision of Walter Gross. There, he examined how the kidneys, heart, muscles, and liver combat various diseases. During this period, his research on chemotherapy brought him the closest in his career to finding a solution for disease.

While doctors commonly prescribe chemotherapy in the 21st century as a treatment for cancer patients, Paul Ehrlich pioneered the technique in the early 1900s.

Like Domagk, Ehrlich was a German doctor who wanted to find better methods to fight diseases. After his initial work with blue dye from the indigo plant, he moved on to studying the effect chemicals have on various physical ailments. During his experiments, Ehrlich often tested the effectiveness of hundreds of chemicals, even poisons, on diseases.

In 1910, Ehrlich crafted a vaccine that kills syphilis microbes without harming the patient. Once called the pox, syphilis is a disease transmitted by sexual intercourse or from an infected mother to her unborn baby. A wavy, very mobile bacteria called a spirochete (spy' re keet) causes the disease. If untreated, an infected person suffers through three distinct phases of deterioration, each more horrible than the last. The first phase involves a small sore. The second phase a few months later involves widespread skin ulcers. Following that, the third phase involves slow destruction of the nerves, blood vessels, bones, and even the brain. The disease usually ends with horrible, incurable and fatal consequences. To treat the illness, Ehrlich tested 605 compounds before finding that dioxy-diamino-arsenobenzene worked. He called the remedy 606 because the compound was the 606th he tested.

Ehrlich's unwillingness to accept failure motivated the young Gerhard. Ehrlich's work with dyes also had a profound impact on Gerhard's later discoveries. While Ehrlich scarcely investigated the dyes' curative properties, Gerhard was nearly 20 years away from discovering how certain dyes could fight bacteria. Unfortunately, before he could do that he needed to find a job that would pay a decent salary. By 1924, Gerhard was not only broke, he was also in love.

Elie Metchnikoff, a Russian bacteriologist, discovered phagocytes in 1882. These are special white blood cells that defend the body by attacking invading bacteria. Metchnikoff influenced Domagk's work in this area.

Chapter 5

Breakthrough

● ●

In 1924, the University of Greifswald hired Gerhard as a privatdocent, or lecturer, in general pathology. While the job was a great honor, it offered no money. To pay his bills, Gerhard continued part time work at the Pathological Institute. It was a difficult time for Gerhard, as he tried to find a better, higher paying position while continuing his research on new techniques to cure disease.

Gerhard began studying the use of x rays to cure carcinomas, a deadly skin cancer, and kidney infections. He made little progress, but continued looking for cancer cures when he accepted a privatdocent position the following year at the University of Münster.

At Münster, Gerhard began examining the role certain white blood cells play in fighting disease. In our bodies, different blood cells serve different purposes. Red blood cells help us breathe while white blood cells defend the body against germs that cause infections. Phagocytes especially interested Gerhard. These are special white blood cells that defend the body by attacking invading bacteria. Elie Metchnikoff, a Russian bacteriologist, influenced Gerhard's work in this area. Metchnikoff discovered these phagocytes in 1882.

While this period of Gerhard's life was educational, it was not fruitful, as *The Journal of Chemical Education* noted in 1954. "Although his researches in this field uncovered some interesting and valuable facts, nothing of immediate curative value resulted," the journal read. In other words, Gerhard's research wasn't leading to cures.

While Gerhard's professional life stagnated, his personal life blossomed. Soon after his arrival in Münster, he married Gertrud Strüde. During their long marriage, the couple had one daughter and three sons: Hildegarde, Gutz, Wolfgang, and Jung.

Meanwhile, Gerhard's investigations into curing disease seemed like little more than endless hours of wasted time. As he conducted various experiments, he barely knew what his next move was going to be. No doubt he was frustrated. He had a new wife, and he was broke. Fortunately, Gerhard's problems were about to disappear.

Much of his work after he graduated from medical school was for free, either as a teacher or researcher. However, he did not work in vain. He was about to receive a pay off for the time he devoted to learning about various experiments scientists before him conducted and about the methods they used in their attempts to combat disease.

In particular, the work Gerhard did trying to improve upon Ehrlich's research, especially his work with dyes, caught the attention of I.G. Farbenindustrie. The German company had enjoyed decades of success producing chemicals and dyes for the global market. The outbreak of World War I, however, pushed the company in a new direction, and Gerhard was prepared to follow along.

Workers at factories, such as those of I.G. Farbenindustrie, left their jobs to fight in the war. Meanwhile, the British blockade prevented exports, and the manufacturing of dyes was reduced to make way for producing explosives and military gases. I.G. Farbenindustrie's years of success in many ways mirrored the fate of Germany, which following the war found itself struggling against financial turmoil.

"Nothing seemed capable of slowing down the prodigious growth rate," as the company web site reads, "but in fact the first shadows were drifting across the auspicious scene, heralding dangers that those involved were slow to recognize ... the outbreak of the First World War, which in August 1914 transformed Europe into a battlefield of previously unknown ferocity and also wreaked immense damage on the development of the chemical industry."

To bounce back from the changes during World War I, I.G. Farbenindustrie merged in 1925 with Bayer, a company that gained worldwide success by developing aspirin in 1899. By the time of the merger, Bayer was the most popular pain reliever on the globe. Unfortunately, following the merger, sales continued to decline. Company officials realized they needed to expand their business beyond just chemicals.

In 1927, a fellow professor at the University of Münster approached Gerhard about working for Bayer. In addition to his academic work, Heinrich Hoorlein was head of pharmaceutical research at Bayer. He was impressed by Gerhard's research and by the paper he'd published in 1924 on infection and chemotherapy. Hoorlein also shared Gerhard's belief that certain chemicals could be used to combat dangerous bacteria.

When Gerhard was 32 years old, I.G. Farbenindustrie hired him as director of its research laboratory in the areas of experimental pathology and bacteriology. The job offered a stable salary and prestige, but most importantly to Gerhard it gave him a chance to focus on discovering better chemical treatments for illnesses that bacteria causes. The doctor took a leave of absence from the University of Münster and began working tirelessly at his new job.

For five years, Gerhard tested thousands of different dyes. He focused on azo dyes that shared a particular group of atoms. Greek philosopher Democritus first described atoms in 400 B.C. as a hard particle of matter, so small they could never be divided. Atom is from the Greek word atomos, which means that which can not be split. Atoms are so small that billions of them can fit on the tip of a pencil. Atoms make up everything in the universe from the ground we stand on to the computers we type on. Atoms make up the air we breathe and the water we drink.

Atomic substances that can't be broken down any further are called elements. Elements have only one type of atom. For example, gold elements contain only gold atoms and hydrogen elements contain only hydrogen atoms. When atoms combine they form molecules. Water molecules, for example, are composed of one atom of oxygen with two atoms of hydrogen. Most dyes contain a hydrogen atom. The dyes Gerhard focused on belonged to a group of atoms known as the sulfonamide group, commonly called sulfas.

Gerhard began by testing various dyes' effectiveness on bacteria collected in a test tube. One of the dyes he tested was a red azo dye that chemist Fritz Mietzsch and Joseph Klarer had formulated. Initially, the dye was marketed as a stain for leather. It was considered superior to other dyes because it bonded so well. In reading about the experiments Mietzsch and Klarer conducted, Gerhard wondered if red azo dye would stick to bacteria as well as it stuck to leather.

In a later speech, Gerhard thanked Mietzsch and Klarer for their contributions to his work, saying, "The problem of chemotherapy on bacterial infections could be solved neither by the experimental research worker, nor by the chemist alone but by the two working together, in very close cooperation over many years."

In his tests, Gerhard quickly discovered red azo dye showed a small effect against the growth of the bacterial organism. Before that, tests showed dyes were not effective as drugs in fighting bacteria. They only were effective in fighting infections much larger organisms caused.

The discovery was quite a break through, but Gerhard realized he needed more proof. In mid-December of 1932, he took the next step and began experimenting with laboratory mice, infecting 26 of them with the *Streptococcus pyogenes* bacteria. Nearly 90 minutes later, he injected 12 of the infected mice with a dye that was sold under the brand name Prontosil. The other 14 mice he left untreated.

The results were amazing. Within four days the untreated mice died of infection. The treated mice didn't. The results seemed indisputable. I. G. Farbenindustrie began clinical testing of the dye on dozens of laboratory animals. Prontosil seemed to work. Despite his break through, Gerhard hesitated. No one is sure exactly why, but he didn't work to produce the drug as a treatment. He didn't conduct experiments on people, and he waited several years to publish his findings.

Some believe Gerhard hesitated because he was using the same formula as the one for leather dye, which means he couldn't take out a patent on it. A patent prevents anyone other than the discoverer from copying, manufacturing or selling the product without permission. Perhaps Gerhard hoped to discover his own chemical formula, one just different enough from Prontosil that he could patent it in his own name.

While many reasons may have delayed Gerhard from publishing the results of his testing, only one thing persuaded him to change his mind. A little girl became very sick, and Gerhard was her last hope. He was also her father.

Gerhard Domagk is in his laboratory, where, in 1927, he began to test a series of new dyes made by I.G. Farbenindustrie as drugs against streptococcal infections in mice.

Chapter 6
Sulfa Saves

● ●

The discovery made by Gerhard and a pair of chemists from I.G. Farbenindustrie was about to change the lives of millions, not just in their homeland, but across the globe. Pneumonia, a lung disease caused by infection, killed nearly 100,000 people a year in the United States alone. Other bacterial infections destroyed millions of lives each year as well, infections such as puerperal sepsis, a blood poisoning that kills mothers in childbirth; cerebrospinal meningitis, a bacterial inflammation of the membranes that envelopes the brain and spinal cord; and gonorrhea, a sexually transmitted bacterial infection that is difficult to treat.

The work that would lead to a life-saving treatment for these and many other diseases began with a needle. In November of 1935, six-year-old Hildegarde Domagk accidentally pricked herself. The prick was a small matter, something that happens to kids all the time. Unfortunately, the needle was loaded with the streptococcal bacteria. The infection quickly spread, reaching the little girl's lymph nodes. Doctors lanced the infection over a dozen times, trying to save her life.

Doctors approached her father and offered an alternative. They wanted to amputate her arm. Even then, they weren't sure she'd survive. Gerhard faced a tough decision. He realized his daughter was suffering from the same type of infection he'd treated with the Prontosil. He never had tried the drug on a person before. In fact, he was fairly certain it wouldn't work, but he had very little to lose.

By this time, another German doctor had reported the effects of Prontosil on an infant suffering from a staph infection in May of 1933. Still, the treatment was not in use. Gerhard decided to proceed anyway. He gave his daughter Prontosil, and much to his relief, it worked. Hildegarde quickly recovered.

Gerhard realized then how important his discovery was, and how many lives could be saved. That same year, he published the results of his experiments with mice in the *Deutsche Medizinische Wochenshrift* in an article entitled "A Contribution to the Chemotherapy of Bacterial Infections." He never mentioned his daughter's case in the article, but that didn't matter.

Colleagues initially received the article with skepticism. The following year, the British Medical Research Council and the American Medical Association validated Prontosil's effectiveness in their own independent research. Finally, other scientists accepted how valuable the treatment was.

As the publication *Nature* noted in November of 1939, "It had almost come to be assumed that bacterial infections were beyond the reach of chemotherapy." In other words, before Prontosil some doctors could offer little more than comfort to their patients while bacterial infections ran their course, often with fatal results.

For all of its benefits, Prontosil had one problem. In many ways, it worked on a patient the same way it worked on a leather belt. It bonded well with bacteria, stopping its spread. Unfortunately, it also turned skin bright red. At the Pasteur Institute, Daniele Bovet along with a number of other scientists began working on solving the problem. They discovered they could divide the drug into two parts. One part included the chemical that dyed skin and leather red. The other part included the sulfonamide or sulfa.

In later experiments, scientists proved the sulfa was effective in preventing the spread of infections that cause a variety of diseases, including pneumonia, puerperal sepsis, cerebrospinal meningitis, and gonorrhea. Sulfa was also far

Dr. Daniele Bovet (left) of the Pasteur Institute was awarded the Nobel Prize for Medicine in 1957. Dr. Boris Chain (right) won the same prize in 1945.

cheaper to produce than Prontosil. Unfortunately, I. G. Farbenindustrie did not have exclusive rights to produce sulfa, so other manufacturers made the drug as well. In fact, sulfa was produced by the ton as a chemical by-product in dye manufacturing. In some ways, Gerhard's hesitation cost his company a fortune.

Still, the end result of Gerhard's discovery was positive. The result saved lives. While his paper was widely read, sulfa received its greatest publicity when a streptococcic infection made Franklin Delano Roosevelt, Jr., son of the U.S. president, deathly ill. Doctors used Prontosil to treat the ailment, and Roosevelt recovered completely.

The men and women who treated the sick immediately recognized the miracle of Gerhard's discovery. Sulfa stopped infection. It saved lives. And very soon it would be needed in quantities unimaginable. During the first several years of production in the United States, sulfa quantities increased from more than 350,000 pounds in 1937 to more than 10 million in 1942.

As demand for sulfa grew, Gerhard continued his experiments. Meanwhile, Germany experienced rapid change. Adolf Hitler, a failed house painter and soldier, tried to overthrow the Bavarian government in 1923. After serving nine months in jail, Hitler began gaining popularity and power. Hitler's Nazi party was anti-Semitic, or discriminated against Jewish people. Hitler and his supporters in their speeches blamed the Jews for the many problems Germany faced. Hitler's organization found support among Germans by promising to restore the national pride lost after World War I. Hitler's supporters pledged to improve the economy by lowering prices and increasing employment. With prices rising rapidly and many Germans out of work, the Nazi message found widespread popular appeal.

In 1932, the Nazis became the largest political party in the Reichstag, the German imperial parliament similar to the U.S. legislature. In 1933, President Paul von Hindenburg appointed Hitler chancellor, or prime minister, of Germany. A few weeks later, a fire destroyed the Reichstag. Although the responsible party was never discovered, many suspected the Nazis themselves.

In response to the fire, the Reichstag gave Hitler emergency dictatorial powers to maintain order. He used the power to form a dictatorship. He eliminated free speech and free press. His opponents quickly were imprisoned, even killed. Hitler's Final Solution called for the eventual extermination of all non-Aryans, such as Jews, Gypsies and

Catholics. During the Nazi reign, more than six million were murdered.

In addition to killing his countrymen, Hitler led the world into a second great war. In February of 1938, Germany and Austria united, violating a post World War I treaty. On September 29th, 1938, England, France and Italy signed the Munich Agreement with Hitler. Many people believed the pact would keep England from going to war with Germany. They were wrong. The agreement gave Nazi Germany control of part of Czechoslovakia. Hitler quickly violated the treaty when his army seized control of the entire country.

Meanwhile, Germany began a massive military build up. Its men were well trained and well equipped. Learning from the tragic battles during World War I, the Germans reinvented warfare with a blitzkrieg approach referred to as lightning war. In combat, German armored tanks, or panzers, penetrated enemy lines and cut off troops. Fast-moving infantry divisions in vehicles then assaulted opposing forces while Stuka dive-bombers destroyed enemy supply lines. With this approach, the Nazis had a war machine that was ready to take on the world, and their first major target was the land of Gerhard's birth.

On September 1, 1939, the German army swept into Poland. Despite having a larger army, the nearly one million Polish soldiers were ill equipped and unprepared. They were quickly defeated. Germany and the Union of Soviet Socialist Republics, which included Russia, divided Poland between them.

The move forced England's Prime Minister Neville Chamberlain to declare war, bringing England into World War II. During the next several years, Germany invaded a number of countries including France, Holland, and eventually Russia. The war cost 55 million lives as the United

Prime Minister Neville Chamberlain brought England into World War II.

States joined the Allied Powers of England, Russia and China and Italy and Japan joined the German Axis.

Despite the awful destruction of World War II, one bright light emerged for Gerhard amid the darkness. From the time following the Japanese attack on Pearl Harbor, when the United States joined the war effort, soldiers were issued sulfa if they got wounded. The effect was remarkable, as Gerhard noted during a speech in the late 1940s, "Whereas in World War I, the U.S. army lost 8.25% of its wounded, by death, in World War II, when sulfonamides were used extensively, only 4.5% died. In World War I, 1.68% of the men reporting sick in the American Army died; now the figure is less than one tenth."

Ironically, sulfa saved Winston Churchill, the Prime Minister of England following Chamberlain. Churchill was widely praised for leadership during much of World War II. He suffered through several bouts with pneumonia, and a sulfa compound cured him.

Although Gerhard's work helped save the lives of millions of famous and everyday people, he encountered few rewards during the reign of Hitler. In fact, he faced a prison sentence when the greatest award a scientist can receive came his way.

Prime Minister Winston Churchill suffered through several bouts of pneumonia. It was sulfa drugs that saved his life.

This is Gerhard Domagk in 1960, when he was 65 years old.

Chapter 7

New Cures

• •

In 1935, the German government imprisoned Carl von Ossietzky, a pacifist who opposed his country's military policies. The next year, he was awarded a Nobel Peace Prize. Hitler responded with a policy that made accepting a Nobel Prize an act of treason.

Four years later, another German citizen won the prize. Gerhard Domagk found out he'd been nominated by British, French and American scientists from countries opposed to the German war effort. When Gerhard discovered he'd won the 1939 Nobel Prize in Physiology or Medicine, he quickly sent a letter of gratitude to the Caroline Medico-Chirurgical Institute in Stockholm, Sweden.

Unfortunately, when the Nazis learned of his correspondence, they took him from his home and held him in jail for more than a week. During his incarceration, the German minister of education wrote another letter declining the prize, and Gerhard was forced to sign it.

Although the Nobel Organization saved Gerhard's medal and diploma, the prize money of $35,000 was given back to the organization after a year. While Gerhard wasn't an active protester against the German government, he wasn't a big supporter either. He focused on his work and labored tirelessly to discover new ways to save lives, even as the Nazi war machine was busy taking them.

"Unfortunately many difficulties stood in the way of our work during and after the war," Gerhard admitted in a speech. "Difficulties with which to some extent we still have to contend. Nevertheless the management of the Bayer Wuppertal-Elberfeld [I. G. Farbenindustrie] dye factories always found ways and means of supporting us - who were engaged in scientific research - indeed they assisted us far more than did the state, whose first duty it should in fact have been to help its citizens, through research, to combat disease."

Despite the Nazi's tactics, Allied forces won the war in Europe, and Gerhard's birthplace, Poland, fell in 1945 under Russian control. The following year, Gerhard's own mother, Martha, was among thousands who were driven from their homes to refuge camps. Despite being a Nobel-prize winning doctor who discovered a life-saving medicine, Gerhard was powerless to help his mother. She died from starvation in a Russian refuge camp.

Meanwhile, U.S. scientists engaged in their own world-changing efforts. They created an atomic bomb, a weapon of incredibly destructive power. On August 6, 1945, the U.S. dropped an atomic bomb over the Japanese city of Hiroshima. That bomb, and the one that followed three days later at Nagasaki vaporized buildings and killed more than 140,000 people in a single blast of heat and light. More people died later from illnesses caused by radiation from the bomb. As a result, Japan surrendered in the summer of 1945.

Two years later, Gerhard finally received his Nobel Prize. More than eight years after he was first notified of the prize, the doctor traveled to Stockholm, Sweden. On December 10, 1947, King Gustaf Adolf VI awarded Gerhard his gold medal and diploma. In his acceptance speech, Gerhard discussed his research work, saying, "I consider it my first duty in the development of chemotherapy to cure those diseases which have hitherto been incurable, so that in the first place those patients are helped who can be helped in no other way."

Even though Gerhard never found another cure besides sulfa for illnesses, he continued working on

*King Gustaf Adolf VI of Sweden is shown here presenting the
1949 Nobel Prize for Physics to Hideki Yukawa.*

tuberculosis and eventually cancer, as he told *Current
Biography 1958.* "I am continuing my work in the field of
chemotherapy, although I know that in all probability I will
never be able to help as many people as will possibly be
annihilated by a single atomic bomb," Gerhard said.

Gerhard's greatest contribution to medicine wasn't
sulfa and the lives it saved, but rather proving to future

Selman Waksman also did important research on antibiotics and developed streptomycin for the treatment of tuberculosis.

scientists that treatments were available for infection. In many ways, the use of sulfa led to greater research and acceptance of other treatments for bacterial infections, such as Selman Waksman's antibiotic streptomycin for tuberculosis and Fleming's penicillin. When Gerhard died of a heart attack in Burgberg, West Germany on April 24,1964, he lacked the world renown of Salk or Fleming. Still, the work Gerhard did was very important.

Today, his drug is gaining wider use for a modern dilemma. In the 1940s, the problem was sulfa only eliminated the spread of bacteria without killing it, thus allowing sulfa-resistant bacteria to continue growing. Today, the problem is some doctors over-prescribe antibiotics. Overuse makes some bacteria resistant to treatment. Sulfa drugs combat this dilemma. They also are widely used for urinary tract and streptococcal infections. Even after his death, Gerhard's work has proved that solutions are possible for all kinds of medical dilemmas.

Alexander Fleming discovered penicillin's antibiotic properties in 1928. It would be 1940 before the penicillin could be made pure enough to be used in the treatment of infection.

Gerhard Domagk Chronology

1895 Gerhard Johannes Paul Domagk is born on October 30, 1895 in Lagow, Germany.

1900 Begins attending scientifically oriented grammar school in Sommerfield.

1914 Enters University of Kiel, enlists in student army during the beginning of World War I, suffers wound at Flanders, joins Medical Corp.

1918 Re-enrolls at University of Kiel.

1921 Receives his M.D. degree and takes a position as an assistant to chemist Ernst Felix Hoppe-Seyler.

1923 Moves to Greifswald and works at the Pathological Institute.

1924 The University of Greifswald hires him as Privatdocent in general pathology, does research on using x-rays to cure disease.

1925 Takes Privatdocent job at the University of Münster, marries Gertrud Strüde, and the couple eventually have one daughter and three sons.

1927 I.G. Farbenindustrie hires as director of its research laboratory in the areas of experimental pathology and bacteriology.

1932 Tests a red azo dye called Prontosil that chemists Fritz Mietzsch and Joseph Klarer formulated. Discovers the dye shows a small effect against the growth of bacterial organisms. Demonstrates Prontosil successfully treats laboratory mice infected with the *Streptococcus pyogenes* bacteria.

1935 Gives six-year-old daughter Hildegarde Prontosil for an infection, and she recovers. Publishes results of experiments in *Deutsche Medizinische Wochenshrift.*

1939 Is awarded Nobel prize in Medicine that Nazis refuse to allow him to accept.

1947 Finally is able to accept Nobel Prize.

1964 Dies of a heart attack April 24 in Burgberg, West Germany.

Antibiotic Timeline of Discovery

500 B.C. First documented use of molds to fight skin infections.

1780s English doctor Edward Jenner discovered vaccination as a means of preventing small pox. Shows injecting weakened bacteria into patients can prevent disease.

1865 Louis Pasteur relates theory to Joseph Lister that specific bacteria causes specific diseases.

1870 A dramatic decline in post-operation infection during surgery in the Franc-Prussian war is credited to Lister's call for clean operating rooms and the use of diluted carbolic acid.

1870s - 1880s German doctor Robert Koch develops bacteriology, a branch of medicine devoted to the study of bacteria.

1882 Russian-French bacteriologist Elie Metchkinkoff observes white blood cells' ability to fight infection.

1908 Chemistry student Paul Gelmo publishes a paper on his work synthesizing *Aminobenzene Sulfonamide* from coal tar to produce a dye.

1910 Paul Ehrlich, who worked with dyes early in his career, crafts a vaccine to fight the bacteria that causes syphilis.

1928 Fleming discovers mold penicillium's antibiotic properties

1932 Chemists Fritz Mietzsch and Joseph Klarer receive a patent for their dye, Prontosil.

1932 Gerhard's experiments with Prontosil shows effectiveness in fighting streptococcal infections in mice.

1935 Gerhard publishes his findings after Prontosil saves the life of his dying daughter. Pasteur Institute scientists led by Daniele Bovet discover sulfa as the active ingredient in Prontosil.

1937 Prontosil saves the life of U.S. president's son, Franklin Delano Roosevelt, Jr.

1937 - 1945 Sulfa widely credited with saving the lives of millions of soldiers and civilians.

1939 René Jules Dubos discovers first antibiotic drug: gramicidin. It works against pneumococcus, staphyloccus, and streptococcus bacteria, but is too dangerous for human use.

1940 Howard Florey and Ernst B. Chain succeed in removing impurities from penicillin and strengthening it

1941 First human tested with penicillin

1941 Dubos' professor, Selman Abraham Waksman begins focusing on the anti-bacterial properties of substances found in soil. He calls these substances antibiotics.

1943 Waksman isolates one antibiotic – streptomycin – that was active against bacteria. Over the next fifteen years he would discover eighteen more antibiotics.

1945 Bacteriologist H. Corwin Hinshaw and pathologist William Hugh Feldman conduct the first clinical trials of streptomycin against tuberculosis (TB). Eventually streptomycin will be used against seventy different types of bacteria which don't respond to penicillin; penicillin made available to the public at the conclusion of World War II

1960s A combination drug of sulfamethoxazole (a sulfonamide) and trimethoprim is proven effective against recurring urinary tract infections and middle ear infections.

2002 Over reliance on antibiotics has led to strains of bacteria that are resistant to this treatment. Increasingly, sulfa is used to treat this. It is also widely used to treat animals.

For Further Reading

While most sources about Gerhard Domagk are written for adults, young adults might enjoy the following:

DeJauregui, Ruth. *100 Medical Milestones That Shaped World History.* San Mateo, California: Bluebird Books, 1998.

On the Web

WWW.Galenet.com
WWW.Nobel.se/Medicine

Glossary

antibiotic—a natural substance that destroys germs

antiseptic—a chemical substance that destroys germs

bacteria—microscopic single-celled organisms; some are dangerous, some are helpful, most are harmless

bacteriologist—scientist who studies bacteria and looks for ways to fight diseases they cause

chemotherapy—use of chemicals to treat disease

infection—a disease germs cause

penicillin—antibiotic molds produce, Alexander Fleming first discovered

Penicillium—a category of fungus

strain—a particular variety or group of microbes

Index